C000246295

BRITAIN IN OLD PHOTOGRAPHS

GALASHIELS

THE OLD GALA CLUB

SUTTON PUBLISHING LIMITED

Sutton Publishing Limited
Phoenix Mill · Thrupp · Stroud
Gloucestershire · GL5 2BU

First published 1996

Front cover: Joseph Brown, bakers.
Back cover: Demolition of Roxburgh Street School, 1971.

British Library Cataloguing in Publication Data
A catalogue record for this book is available from the British Library.

ISBN 0-7509-1316-9

Typeset in 10/12 Perpetua.
Typesetting and origination by
Sutton Publishing Limited.
Printed in Great Britain by
Ebenezer Baylis, Worcester.

A panoramic view of the town from Bruce's Hill in the 1920s, showing New Gala House, the spire of St Paul's mill buildings, the Scottish Woollen Technical College and the railway.

CONTENTS

Cornmill Square in the 1930s, showing the Fountain, War Memorial, Mid Mill to the left and the tower of Old Parish Church at the top of Lawyers Brae on the right. Sited at the foot of Lawyers Brae is a bust commemorating Robert Burns (1759–96). This bust was unveiled on the same day as the Fountain in Cornmill Square, 31 May 1913. The cost of the bust was raised from the proceeds of cycle parades and donations.

INTRODUCTION

It is often assumed by visitors, or by those who come to live from outwith the area, that the town of Galashiels is simply a product of the expansion in the textile industry in the nineteenth century. This is, however, quite untrue. Some of the earliest human habitation sites in the Scottish Borders are to be found in Galashiels Parish, especially at Railway Haugh near Rink Farm where worked flints up to 6,000 years old have been found in considerable number. The area also has examples of Bronze and Iron Age habitation sites, many hill forts and ancient trackways. Within the boundaries of Galashiels Burgh, Bronze Age burial sites have been found at Bow Butts, Gala Park and the Old Town Churchyard. There was an Iron Age fort at Windyknowe and major Iron Age forts at Rink Hill and at Caddon Cliffs. Two of the three brochs in the south of Scotland are within a few miles of the town at Torwoodlee and at Bow Farm. The Romans built, or adapted for their own use, a Celtic shrine at Easter Langlee. A Roman road from the Legion fortress at Newstead (*Trimontium*) passed through Easter Langlee and its temple site, along Netherdale, through the Old Town of Gala, up Manse Street past Blynlee, before crossing to Torwoodlee and above Clovenfords and heading for the upper Tweed Valley forts at Lynn and the Clydesdale area. The present town of Galashiels, and indeed most of its satellite villages, was founded by the Angles who settled in the area in the seventh and eighth centuries under the kings of Bernicia and later of the Old Northumbrian Kingdom. The name Galashiels, 'the dwellings by the Gala', appears to be of eighth-century origin. The original town was a street with cottages and yards on either side running from about The Grange along Church Street to the Old Town Cross with an Anglian manor at the west end. In the Anglo-Norman period there appears to have been a moat just across from St Paul's Church in Scott Crescent.

The Tweed Basin became part of the Kingdom of Scotland in about 1018 but retained its Anglian population, customs, language and ecclesiastical and civil organisations of parishes and shires. Indeed, from this region the parish and shire systems had spread to the rest of Scotland by the early Middle Ages.

Despite the turbulence of periodic warfare with England, during and after the Wars of Independence, Galashiels grew with dwellings along the Loan (now Elm Row and Lawyers Brae) and along Tea Street and the Glebe. After 1320 the Ettrick Forest area, of which Galashiels was a part, was administered by the Earls of Douglas who had a strong tower, known locally as 'Hunters Hall', in Glebe Place. The tower walls were some 7 ft thick, and it was still occupied until 1813 when it was demolished to make way for the Old Town School. During the medieval period there were also settlements within the later Burgh boundaries at Buckholm, Ladhope, the Chingle (where Bank Street and Channel Street now stand), Langhaugh, Langlee, Netherdale and Galabrig.

The Earls of Douglas used the village as an administrative centre for the collection of rents until their exile by the Crown in 1455, when the kings of Scotland became directly responsible for the area. The Pringle family, who had been shield bearers to the Earls of Douglas, obtained the right to be rangers of the Tweed Ward of Ettrick Forest based in Galashiels and became Lairds of the Manor. Gala House in Scott Crescent dates from 1463 when the Laird of Gala, Robert Pringle, and his wife, Elspeth Dishington, a

Bruce heiress, erected the first stone-built tower on the site of the present house. The old Hunters Hall became the King's Fortalice in Galashiels and, as the Scottish Exchequer Records show, it was used to repair and maintain early cannon and bombards used by the Crown in its warfare with England or 'over-mighty subjects' such as the Douglas family. The Estates of Galashiels were subjected to enclosure and the early seventeenth-century Pringle Lairds required their tenants to plant trees as part of their leases or pay larger rents.

In terms of church history there appear to have been Anglian preaching crosses at Kilnknowe and Crosslee on the Gala Water. The first recorded church in the parish, however, was at Lindean which has links with St Cuthbert, the great border saint of the Anglian period. Selkirk Abbey, founded by David I but later transferred to Kelso, may also have been located at Lindean. In the Middle Ages Galashiels village was served by a chapel of ease probably situated in the Old Town Churchyard. By 1617 the parish church had been transferred from Lindean to Galashiels and was rebuilt in that year. All that now remains of the 1617 church is the Scott Aisle (or Gala Aisle), erected in 1636.

Galashiels may have had fulling (or wool processing) mills throughout the Middle Ages as it had swift running streams and plentiful local wool. The first woollen mills recorded were three in 1583 belonging to the Laird of Gala. The village was elevated into a Burgh of Barony in 1599 by Sir James Pringle, who was an MP and courtier at the court of King James VI and I. The town's Tollbooth was erected at this time and the right to hold two annual fairs, as well as a weekly market, was granted to the town. Further rights were conferred on the Burgh in 1617, 1633 and 1697.

The eighteenth century saw a gradual but steady rise in the prosperity and population of the area and an increase in textile development in the Burgh. Close links were forged between some of the local textile

Buckholm Tower, on the slopes of Buckholm Hill overlooking the vale of Gala, showing the barmkin wall and gate, 1930s. The tower is now roofless and in a poor state of preservation. It has not been lived in since the 1930s. The last resident was Bob Brockie, who was born in a box bed in the tower in 1890. He worked as a shepherd on Buckholm Farm.

pioneers and manufacturers in the Yorkshire area where several local apprentices were trained in new techniques. A Cloth Hall to promote trade was erected in 1791 with the assistance of the local parish minister, Dr Robert Douglas, while the writings of Sir Walter Scott popularised the wearing of 'tweeds' by the upper classes and gave a great boost to textile production in the town. Galashiels had, however, only about 4,000 inhabitants until the coming of the railway in 1849. This link to the coalfields of Lothian and to wider markets revolutionised textile trade in the town and by the 1890s the population had grown to almost 20,000. The town's growth was only hindered by its being closely hemmed in by hills which prevented the building of further mills. The Galashiels manufacturers constructed new factories at Selkirk, Earlston, Innerleithen, Peebles and Stow. As a rail junction on the Edinburgh/Carlisle, Peebles/Berwick lines Galashiels developed a considerable service trade and gained a reputation in the nineteenth century for its good quality shops and range of banking and insurance offices. It also serviced a prosperous agricultural hinterland and its annual Agricultural Show was an important event for farmers until the late 1930s.

The imposition of foreign tariffs, particularly the Mackinley tariff imposed by the US Government in 1890, led to a decline in the local textile trade. The late Victorian agricultural depression also had an adverse impact on the town and its neighbourhood. The twentieth century in Galashiels has been marked by a continual decrease in the number of textile mills and in a marked depopulation of the countryside. The town, however, has been restored to its old role as a local administrative centre for both national and local government departments and for many insurance companies and banks. There have been many new housing developments, both public and private. With the establishment of large new residential estates on the outskirts of the town at Langlee and Tweedbank, the town's population in 1995 was about 15,500. In marked contrast to the late nineteenth century, the town now enjoys a clean healthy environment, with good educational and shopping facilities and with ample parks for sporting interests. New educational developments include the Scottish College of Textiles at Netherdale becoming the Faculty of Textiles for Heriot Watt University, and the Borders College in Melrose Road which is now the main centre for further education in the Borders. Major shopping developments are under way in Channel Street and Wilderhaugh with further developments proposed for the Currie Road area of the town. A replacement swimming pool in Livingstone Place was opened in 1984. At Netherdale the local rugby team provides excellent sporting entertainment and continues to supply players for the Scottish team.

Galashiels has, therefore, a long history of which it can be proud. It is a mistake to think that as most of the older buildings still standing are nineteenth century in origin that the town began then. It is rather that the town's Victorian industrialists were so keen to bring in what was new and best that they swept away almost all relics of the past. The surrounding villages such as Stow, Clovenfords and Lindean all exhibit a healthy community spirit and add to the attraction of this part of the central Scottish Borders.

Ian M. Miller, President,
The Old Gala Club.

Members of the Old Gala Club on a visit to Ancrum as part of the Club's 1991 summer programme. The Old Gala Club is the Galashiels and District Local History Association. The club was founded in 1949 and holds the town's museum and photographic collections. The club arranges lectures in Old Gala House and the Volunteer Hall and organises a programme of summer visits to places of historic interest. The club also undertakes local history research projects.

STREET SCENES

At one time the High Street was a busy thoroughfare full of shops open until late in the evening. The general layout of this street has altered little since this picture was taken in about 1905. The tall building with cupola in the centre was built in 1888 for the Galashiels Co-operative Store Company. Our photographs depict a variety of architectural styles including traditional terraced houses and post-war prefabricated temporary dwellings. Most scenes are traffic free, not congested as they are today.

Post-war prefabricated houses in Larchbank Street, 1960s. These were demolished in the mid-1980s and replaced with modern brick-built houses, constructed for Eildon Housing Association.

James Paton delivering milk for the Co-op in Meigle Street, early 1900s. Houses now continue up towards Mossilee.

Abbotsford Road, now part of the busy A7, *c.* 1912. Eastlands Park to the right, now the Public Park, was gifted to the town by the Scotts of Gala and opened in 1885.

Scott Street brae, *c.* 1875. Note the gap where houses have still to be built. These houses have now been modernised, although externally are very similar.

The lower part of Overhaugh Street looking towards Market Street, showing the unemployment office (the broo) and Melrose the bakers.

The first concrete-built terrace in the town, including the Ayrshire Market and Tony's Fish Bar, c. 1950. The 'concretes' were built in the 1870s and demolished in the 1960s to be replaced with local authority housing.

Top of Paton Street showing late nineteenth-century housing, part of Mid Mill and the forecourt of Purves' Garage, 1930s. Mid Mill is on the site of a fulling mill that existed in 1585.

A horse being watered in High Buckholmside. This is now the busy A7, although otherwise little changed.

Textile workers' houses in Tweed Place, later renamed Duke Street, with Waukrigg Mill to the rear.

Junction of High Street, Bank Street and Overhaugh Street, 1912.

St John Street, showing the triumphal arch erected for the coronation festivities of Edward VII, which were held in the town on Saturday 9 August 1902. The arch, designed by Mr Goodsir, was described as being 'full of artistic merit'.

Children in the snow, St John Street. The gates to the rear now lead to the Scott Park but were originally the main gates to Gala House, which was demolished in 1985.

Church Street, with its nineteenth-century buildings lining what is the oldest street in Galashiels, 1960s. School Lane is mid-way on the right, once leading to the Old Town School which was erected in 1813 and demolished in 1937. The school was on the site of Hunter's Hall, a fourteenth-century stronghold of the Earls of Douglas.

Tea Street contains a row of cottages, seventeenth century in origin. These are the oldest surviving inhabited dwellings in the town and were thatched until earlier this century. The long strips of garden ground behind the cottages were once 'cottars' yards'. In the distance is the spire of Old Parish and St Paul's Church.

SHOPS & BUILDINGS

Since the turn of the century many prominent buildings in the town have either been demolished or used for other purposes. At one time there were over twenty woollen mills but owing to a decline in the trade most of these have disappeared. The British Linen Bank, shown here in the High Street in the 1950s, has accommodated various businesses but the frontage has altered little. The adjacent East Church, now St Ninian's, once had railings to the front.

An early photograph of Adam Purves' blacksmith shop in Damside.

Adam Purves' garage, shop and office staff in Market Street, 1930s. The gentleman on the right is Mr Adam Purves.

A. Tait, butchers, 98 High Street. The business ceased trading in about 1920. There was also a shop in Galapark at the top of Scott Street, later occupied by a shoemaker, then by Border Domestics.

J. Inglis, grocers, Market Street, *c.* 1908.

Willie Welsh outside his bookseller/stationers at 58 High Street.

At one time there were a number of 'house shops' in the town. This was a 'sweetie shop' owned by Miss Lawrie at 103 Scott Street from 1916 until the 1940s.

Commercial Hotel, Bridge Street, which became the Maxwell Hotel and is now the premises of Scottish Borders Enterprise. The hotel was, for many years in the late nineteenth century, the home of William Reavley – a local inventor who won a gold medal at the Liverpool International Exhibition of 1894.

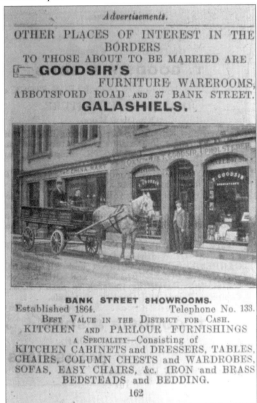

This advertisement for Thos Goodsir and Son, house furnishers, shows their showrooms at 37 Bank Street in about 1905.

Staff outside Locke's Drapery Emporium, Channel Street (Tel. Galashiels 149), *c.* 1930. A lady's blouse could be purchased for 3*s* 11*d* and a nightdress for 5*s* 11*d*. The premises are now occupied by MacKay's Fashion Store.

Gebbie's Garage, Channel Street, *c.* 1939. This is now the Co-op Funeral and Monumental Services. The photograph also shows The Thistle Café.

G. Henry, bakers, Channel Street, 1920s. The premises are now occupied by Supercard.

Market Square, with drinking trough. The ornate lamp standard now stands in Tweed Crescent. The old police station is the small low building next to the Railway Inn.

Capitol Cinema, *c.* 1970. The Capitol started life as The Playhouse and opened on 11 May 1920 with a production of *The Mikado* by Galashiels Amateur Operatic Society. It has undergone several name changes over the years. After complete refurbishment it reopened in 1995 as a four screen multiplex, The Pavilion.

The interior of the original Pavilion Cinema in Channel Street with its murals and fire curtain displaying advertising for local businesses. The Pavilion was demolished in 1970.

Construction of the War Memorial and Municipal Buildings, *c.* 1924. A commemorative cornerstone was laid on 3 December 1924 in the presence of HRH the Prince of Wales. The memorial was opened by Earl Haig of Bemersyde on 4 October 1925. The tower was designed by Sir Robert Lorimer in the likeness of a border peel tower. In front stands the 'Border Reiver', a bronze figure armed and on horseback, the work of Thomas J. Clapperton, sculptor.

The demolition of Roxburgh Street School, 1971. The school, which opened in 1894, had been closed since 1964. The ambulance station was later constructed on the site.

The Town Hall, *c.* 1914. Built in 1869 and purchased by the Town Council in 1920, it was demolished in 1969. The Volunteer Hall, St John Street, had been acquired in 1963 as a suitable alternative public hall. The people of Galashiels used to meet under the clock of the Town Hall to bring in the New Year.

South of Scotland Central Technical Training College was erected in 1909 on the site of Victoria Mill at a cost of over £21,000; it later became the Scottish College of Textiles and was relocated at Netherdale in the 1960s. This building is now known as Government Buildings, and houses the Inland Revenue, VAT, and employment services.

Robert Richardson jnr outside the premises of Robert Richardson and Son, Tweed Merchants, 120 Galapark Road, *c.* 1927. The firm later moved to 94 Galapark Road 'where the four roads meet', which had belonged to F. Lynn & Son cabinet makers and later the Reiver Gallery. The Morris Cowley (KS 549) belonged to Robert Richardson snr.

The reopening of the Cottage Hospital by the Earl of Dalkeith, after refurbishment and the installation of electric lighting, 15 September 1923.

Waukmillhead Mill was erected between 1799 and 1802, and occupied the site of one of the fulling mills belonging to Gala Estate in 1585. The mill was demolished in 1949 and the site became part of Bank Street Gardens.

Mid Mill opposite the Territorial Hall in Paton Street. Mid Mill was built on the site of one of the earliest mills in Galashiels, the Middle Waulk Mill. Mid Mill was demolished in 1953 but the run for the water wheel was retained as a feature.

Comelybank Mill, demolished for development in spring 1996, with King Street in the background and the track of the Waverley line in the foreground.

Botany Mill with the Glassite Congregation meeting house, known as the Kail Kirk, in the right foreground. The Glassites were an independent religious sect.

Buckholm Mill with the footbridge over the River Gala leading to Mill Park. The mill was built in 1846 on the site of a cornmill which had been destroyed by fire in 1839. An extension on the right bank of the River Gala was built in 1882. Electricity was installed in 1884.

Abbotsview, originally a private house named Lynhurst, was built in 1872 and belonged to Walter Cochrane, mill owner. The house was extended and became the Co-op Convalescent Home until it was demolished in 1984. The site was then developed as a private housing estate.

CHILDREN & YOUTH ORGANISATIONS

The photograph introducing this section shows the pupils of Old Town School in about 1890. This school was demolished in 1937. We have shown other school groups, including the girls of St Trinnean's evacuated to the town from Edinburgh during the Second World War and a selection of youth organisations. The photographs cover the period 1890 to 1960.

Pupils of St Peter's School, 1923/4. The school, which opened in 1859, succeeded Episcopalian schools in Wilderhaugh, then Old Gala House, and was a private establishment under the authority of the adjoining Scottish Episcopal Church. It was later taken over by the local authority but retains a link with the church, the rector acting as school chaplain.

Pupils of St Peter's School outside the church hall, 1913.

Victoria Park Junior Sports, *c.* 1920. The Victoria Park was acquired from Gala Estate in 1896 and named in commemoration of Queen Victoria's Diamond Jubilee the following year. It was officially opened as a public park in June 1901.

Pupils from the Burgh School on a visit to Bowhill, the home near Selkirk of the Duke of Buccleuch. The Burgh School was opened in 1874 to accommodate children from the rapidly developing Gala Park area of the town.

A group of pupils from St Trinnean's School after visiting an exhibition of dolls in Old Gala House. The school was evacuated from Edinburgh to New Gala House during the Second World War.

Dolls made by Miss Burnet, assistant teacher at Galapark School, on display in the window of Galashiels Gas Light Co., 1916. The dolls were photographed and postcards produced for sale in aid of the wartime Comforts Fund.

Pupils of Lindean School, 1906/7. The school log book records that on 5 January 1874 the attendance was small on account of measles being in the district, and on 17 March 1911 pupils were given a holiday as the school had to be washed out for a concert and dance being held in the evening. The proceeds of this event were to provide a coronation picnic for the children. The sum of £2 2s was raised. The school finally closed on 30 March 1961 because of the small number of pupils.

Pupils from St Peter's School attending St Peter's Church on St Ninian's Day, 1957. The schoolhouse and part of the original school buildings dating from about 1859 are in the background.

The Scott family, Halliburton: a Galashiels family in about 1914.

Galashiels Baby Show at a Child Welfare Exhibition in the Town Hall opened by Lady Polwarth, 11 August 1917. These shows boosted morale following food rationing and the German U-boat campaign against British shipping.

Pupils of Galashiels Academy primary department, 1954. The primary department was housed in 'The Hut', a temporary building, for many years. The Academy's striped blazer was designed in the 1930s.

Galashiels Academy prefects and Rector Mr William A. Forbes, late 1950s. Mr Forbes was rector from 1942 until 1962.

Braw Lad Laurie Grant and Braw Lass Margaret Finlay visiting Glendinning Terrace School, 1953. This school, formerly in the Parish of Melrose, was built in 1876 by the Melrose School Board. It was taken over by the Burgh School Board in 1891 and rebuilt in 1936.

Braw Lad Bill Keddie and Braw Lass Maureen Tully visiting St Peter's School in 1956.

The opening chorus at a children's concert.

Standing room only on the new roundabout at the Public Park, *c.* 1958.

Camping out in Scott Street in about 1918 are Tom Waddell, Robert Douglas, Alex Patterson, Billy Redpath, Willie Sommerville and Alex Chalmers, with Kemp the dog.

Fishing for minnows in the River Tweed at Glenmayne Haugh, 1930.

A group of Brownies enjoying 'Brownie Revels' at Netherdale, *c.* 1955.

Guides from the 2nd Company of Galashiels Guides receiving their Queen's Guide award, the first in Selkirkshire, in September 1956. Left to right: Isobel Anderson, Miss Margaret Ritchie (District Commissioner), Irene Kirkpatrick, Mrs Jean Kemp (County Commissioner), Marion Harding, Miss Freda Robertson (Captain 2nd Gala), Norma Kirkpatrick and Louise Brown.

March past of Gala Boys Brigade companies in Bank Street, 1950s.

St Peter's Boys Brigade with their chaplain Leslie Dover and president Jimmy Miller, 1955. This 3rd Galashiels Company was founded in 1908.

Boys Brigade camp, Gosford, 1911.

1st Galashiels Scout Troop, with Robert S. Hayward presenting the county flag, 1952. The scout hall in St John Street is now called the Hayward Scout Centre.

St Paul's Lifeboys, March 1934.

St Paul's Lifeboys, 'The Steadies', with the Revd Alec Innes, April 1934.

TRANSPORT

In this section we have included various forms of transport from the horse and gig to steam locomotives, early hard tyre cars, lorries and charabancs. Photographs are also shown of the Waverley railway line which closed in 1969. This scene of Boleside in the early 1900s shows popular modes of transport of that era. The railway line is the branch line from Galashiels to Selkirk; this opened in 1856, closed to passenger traffic in 1951 and continued for freight only until finally closing in 1964.

Party in gig outside Bridge House, Bridge Place, *c.* 1890.

Co-op milk cart in Channel Street, *c.* 1920.

Galashiels railway station with the Scottish Woollen Technical College in the background, *c.* 1965. The railway reached Galashiels in 1848. The North British Railway Co. officially chose Waverley Route as the name of this line as it passed within a mile of Abbotsford, home of Sir Walter Scott. Many of the locomotives had names associated with works by Scott.

Willie Gow and staff with the 'Coffee Pot' engine on the Jubilee run of the Galashiels to Selkirk branch line, 5 April 1906.

Galashiels stationmaster's house and the timetable board. The station bridge to the left was opened by Miss J.S. Mercer on 29 June 1938.

The weighbridge at Galashiels station. Galashiels Health Centre, which was opened on 29 July 1983 by John Gibb Esq., OBE, MA, LLB, the chairman of the Borders Health Board, now occupies this site.

A diesel heading south on the Waverley Line below Langlee, 1960s. The railway line has been made into a walkway known as the 'black path'.

The Waverley Line disappearing under bridge no. 100 at Low Buckholmside, 1971. This line which linked Edinburgh with Carlisle closed in 1969. Laidlaw and Fairgrieve's Mill and the siding for Brownlee's Timber Merchants are to the right. This photograph was taken from the bridge at Kennedy's Brae, now demolished.

Charabancs in Market Square, 1920s.

The bus station in Market Square, 1950s. Supporters queue for the bus to Melrose for the rugby sevens or 'sports' as they were known. In 1965, owing to traffic congestion, Scottish Omnibuses had to transfer their operations to Stirling Street.

Newcastle to Glasgow bus in collision with a touring bus in Clovenfords, *c.* 1925.

The bus shelter for visitors to Peel Hospital, *c.* 1950. The hospital closed in April 1988 following the opening of Borders General Hospital near Melrose.

LS 102, belonging to Mr James Brown of Netherby, Galashiels, at Langhaugh House, 1906.

LS 36, a three-wheeled car (motor tricycle) constructed by Mr Messer, builder, Galashiels.

The Central Motor Showrooms with the brick-built Playhouse cinema to the rear.

'On the buses'. Aly Cunningham, Peter Cuthbertson, Archie Stewart and Mac McDonald awaiting passengers in Market Square, 1927/8.

Horse-drawn snowplough at the top of Overhaugh Street, 29 December 1906.

Snowplough in Livingstone Place, 1963.

The lorry of J. Dick & Son, Bank Street, 1910. This was a conversion from a Humber motor car to a van by Adam Purves & Son.

John Arnott, contractor, with his flat-bed lorry loaded with wool sacks, locally known as 'sheets', c. 1920.

James Waddell and his belt-driven Ariel, LS 350, 1914.

A lorry which skidded off the road in Langlee housing estate, 1968.

PEOPLE AT WORK

In the nineteenth and twentieth centuries, the woollen industry was predominant in the town. Shown here are workers at 'Hunter's Mill', originally Abbotsford Mill and now Waverley Mill. Galashiels is also at the meeting point of several routes; therefore the town has always been a shopping centre for the central Borders. This is illustrated in photographs showing shop, transport, office and domestic staff and trades such as stonemasons and cobblers.

A warper at work in a Galashiels textile mill.

Workers at Wakefield Mill (R. and A. Sanderson): Jimmy Dickson, Andrew Fox, and Bob Young.

Hall & Co. steeplejacks at work at
Bridge Mill, Huddersfield Street,
June 1908.

Seamstresses believed to be at J. and J.C. Dorward's Waukrigg Mill, *c.* 1906/7.

Fleshers at Sanderson and Murray, Wilderhaugh, known locally as 'the skinworks', *c.* early 1900s.

Cobblers at Charlie Hogarth, shoemaker, Store Close, Bank Street, with Charlie Hogarth in the centre, early 1900s.

A group of sculptors standing in front of the Royal Coat of Arms, which they have prepared for the post office building. The town's new head post office opened in its Channel Street location in 1896.

G. Sutherland & Sons, monumental sculptors, Albert Place, from the vantage point of Lawyers Brae.

Landslide at Ladhope railway tunnel. On Thursday 14 December 1916, the embankment collapsed in Ladhope Vale, blocking the Waverley Line for twelve days. A single line was resumed between Kilnknowe Junction and Galashiels North signal cabin. Traffic on both lines resumed on Friday 7 June 1918. The new wall built was 323 feet long and 26 feet high, with another wall 300 feet long behind, supporting the High Road.

Workmen on the Waverley line using a lifting jack, before the First World War.

Tweed Vineries, Clovenfords, 1920s. This was established in 1869 by William Thomson, head gardener to the Duke of Buccleuch. The vineries produced 12,000 to 14,000 lb of grapes (including 'Gros Colman', 'Muscat of Alexandra' and 'Black Alicante') annually. The grapes were mainly grown for the London market. In addition there were glasshouses for the cultivation of plants and flowers to supply Thomson's florist shop in Castle Street, Edinburgh. These were sent by rail to Edinburgh daily.

Boyd's Cycle Depot, Market Street, *c.* 1900. This was the first motor agent in the town. James M. Boyd started dealing in cars and motor cycles in the late 1890s. The business ceased trading in 1905.

J. Brown, bakers, with J. Thomson, Miss Dick, Miss Irvine, Robert Brown and J. Brown.

Myra Templeton in the lingerie department of Galashiels United Co-op Society, 119 High Street, 1950s.

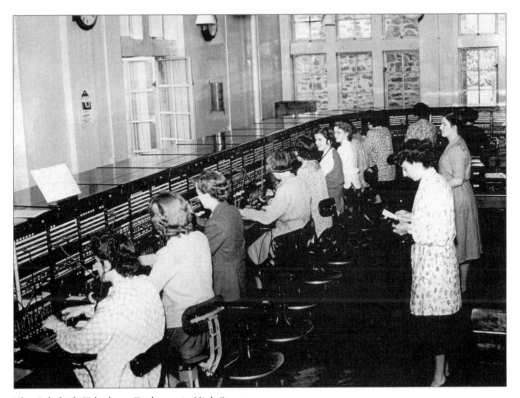

The Galashiels Telephone Exchange in High Street.

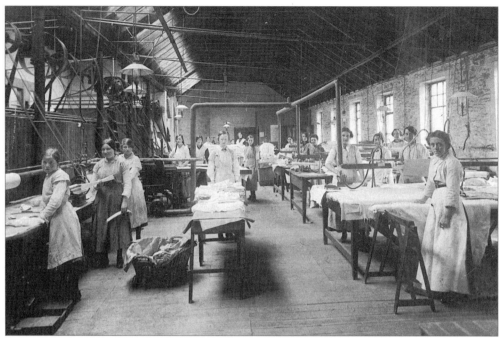

Hillside Laundry, above the Edinburgh Road, early 1900s. The premises later became a creamery of the Border Co-operative Society.

Domestic staff at St Peter's Rectory, c. 1890. At that time there were also two gardeners, who are not in this photograph. The rector's wife, Mrs Jenkins, was a keen gardener and opened the garden several times a year to raise funds for the Chanda Mission in India and for work among the urban poor.

Traction engine towing a boiler in Market Street, *c.* 1920.

Workers laying sewers in Hill Street, 1908.

James Smart, policeman, *c.* 1860.

Postal workers: Davie Todd, Jim Patterson, Alex Ruddiman, Bert Gladstone and Messrs Nicholson, Crosbie, Donald, Houghton, and Porteous.

Governors of Galashiels Gas Light Co., 1950: James McPherson Brown, Mr Dow (former gas manager), Alex Fairgrieve, W.C. Campbell (gas manager), D.G. Stalker and A.P. Dorward.

Office staff take time off to have their photograph taken, *c.* 1920.

William Smith, while apprenticed to Cartwright, a chemist in Bank Street, Galashiels, before becoming pharmacist with Galashiels United Co-op Society. Mr Smith later became chairman of the Borders Co-operative Society, chairman of Galashiels Local Relief Committee and a special constable.

James M. Waddell, staff photographer with the *Border Telegraph*.

CHURCH & CHURCH ACTIVITIES

Until the 1960s, in Galashiels as elsewhere, the churches played a major part in the life of a great many of the population. This section starts with a view of the Scott or Gala Aisle in the old churchyard, which is all that remains of the seventeenth-century parish church of Galashiels. The Aisle was restored and re-roofed in 1992. The old churchyard contains several interesting memorials, including the family tomb of the African explorer Mungo Park. Other photographs show groups of clergy, church events and organisations, and some of the church buildings in the town.

Old Parish and St Paul's Church showing the memorial door, and the iron railings which were removed during the Second World War. This red sandstone building was constructed in 1876–81, the architects being Hay and Henderson of Edinburgh and J. & J. Hall of Galashiels. Known as St Paul's Church, it opened for worship on 23 November 1881. After the closure of the parish church in 1931 it became Old Parish and St Paul's Church.

Old Parish Church choir, with choirmaster A. MacLachlan, 1914.

Ministers from the churches in Galashiels, 1935.

Opening of St Mark's Church sale,
25 March 1939. Miss Anna Buchan
(the novelist O. Douglas), sister of
John Buchan, Lord Tweedsmuir, is
being presented with a bouquet of
tulips by Olive Noble while the Revd
Mr and Mrs Brisby look on.

West Parish Church choir at the wedding of G. Sanderson, owner of Botany Mill, to M. Dalgetty.

Borders Mission Festival held at St Peter's Church, late 1950s. Bishop Warner, of the diocese of Edinburgh, is in attendance. The St Peter's choir and servers are to the fore and the Rector of Galashiels (Leslie Dover), of Jedburgh (George Martineau) and of Melrose (Henry Kelsey) are on the right of the photograph.

The Revd George H. Donald and family, 1924. Mr Donald, an army chaplain during the First World War, was minister of St Paul's before emigrating to Montreal, Canada, in January 1925. One son, James, became an actor and appeared in many films during the 1950s and 1960s including *Bridge on the River Kwai*.

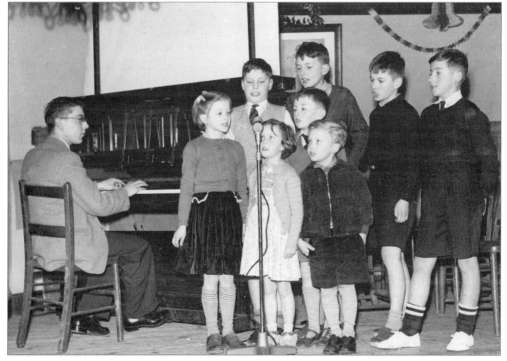

Young performers at a Christmas concert in St Peter's Church Hall, 1957. The pianist is Drew Patterson, an officer in the 3rd Galashiels Boys Brigade.

A Salvation Army wedding at East Church, 9 May 1936. The bridegroom was Captain Ronald Chalker, Galashiels, and the bride was Lieutenant Marjory Smith, Portobello.

The wedding of J. Morrison and May Fairgrieve in the gardens of Bridge House (now Ballencrieff), Bridge Street, *c.* 1899.

Young Wives Group party at St Peter's Rectory, January 1955. Mrs Connie Dover, the rector's wife, is third from the left in the back row.

Mothers' Union party in the upper hall at St Peter's Church, 1957. The hall, which was erected in 1887, had a church officer's house and smaller meeting rooms on the lower floor, and was used by many organisations.

Ladhope Parish Church, later converted to a fitness club. This was the first church in Galashiels to have an organ installed. The introduction of music did not meet with the approval of all the congregation and some members left the church.

Church of Our Lady and St Andrew, with its primary school on the left. The school, which opened in this building in 1897, was demolished in about 1989 to make way for Ladhope Vale Bypass. The replacement school, St Margaret's RC Primary, had opened in 1968.

West Parish Church play, *c.* 1913.

Halliburton Mission summer outing, June 1913. A party of approximately fifty enjoyed a delightful drive to Cowdenknowes, near Earlston. After a hearty tea the party was taken round the house and gardens. They then enjoyed games and walks by the riverside before returning to Galashiels at about 10 p.m.

Site of St Mary's Scottish Episcopal Chapel and School, Wilderhaugh, opened 1851. The first curate was the Revd Thomas Augustus Purdie from Glasgow. From 1854 he was the first rector of St Peter's Church, Galashiels.

Ladhope Free Church, now Hergé's Bistro, Island Street. In 1885 this church building was considered by the congregation to be too small and was replaced by a new building, St Andrew's Church, in Bridge Street.

SPORT & RECREATION

The game of rugby football has played a prominent part in the lives of the people of Galashiels, and Gala RFC has produced several internationalists. This photograph shows players from the first Gala rugby side of 1875 at a commemorative dinner held in 1935. Another shows the six Gala players who played for Scotland in 1971. A wide selection of other sports such as swimming, bowling, football, curling on the River Tweed and the more leisurely pastime of draughts are also shown.

Galashiels Public Baths, Wilderhaugh, were opened on 13 September 1915 and gifted to the town by Mr and Mrs A. Anderson Dickson.

Ladies of Galashiels Swimming Club, 1930s. Gala Swimming Club was formed in October 1915. Gents attended on Mondays and ladies on Thursdays. The following year the Town Council agreed that club members could be admitted each evening after 6.30 p.m. at an admission charge of tuppence for adults and a penny for juveniles.

A gymnastics display at St Peter's Church hall, 1913.

Gala Harriers, instituted in 1902, outside the Burgh School before their inter-club run with the then famous West of Scotland Harriers, January 1908. The route lay via Seven Trees, Brunswick Hill, Netherbarns, Gas Works and home by Langlee. After the run the visitors entertained the local runners.

Netherdale Mills tennis courts with a match in progress, early 1920s.

St Paul's Church badminton club, 1950s.

Gala veterans versus Selkirk veterans cricket match at Mossilee, in aid of Soldiers' Comforts Fund, 10 July 1915.

Galashiels Ladies Golf Club versus Australians, 2 July 1919. The Australians were on war service and billeted in Galashiels. Following the event prizes were presented to Miss Hogarth and Mr Robertson.

Gala Waverley Cycling Club, *c.* 1890. The club was formed in 1884 and had its headquarters at James Boyd, cycle dealers, Market Street, until 1905.

Cyclists taking part in the Milk Race, Lee Brae, 1960s.

Gala Angling Association liberating spawn at
Cascade Burn, May 1947. The Association was
founded in 1860 and from an early date was
involved in improving the natural fish stock. In
1912 it opened its own trout hatchery.

Galashiels Draughts Club, winners of the Border League Championship Cup, 1905/6. Teams from
Galashiels, Peebles, Selkirk, Walkerburn and Clovenfords took part in the Border League. Matches were
played on a Saturday. Two points were awarded for a win and one point for a draw. Any team unable to
fulfil an arranged match forfeited two points to the opposing team.

Galashiels Academy Former Pupils Ladies Hockey Team, 1930/1.

Galashiels Ladies Hockey Team at a game in the Scott Park to celebrate their new outfits, 1963. The material for the skirts was supplied by Arthur Armstrong, Bank Street, at 28s per yard.

Boys' five-a-side football competition in the Public Park, 1960s.

Gala Fairydean, winners of the King Cup with their 3–1 victory over Berwick Rovers at Duns, April 1961.

Gala Bowling Club, 1945. Mrs William Bruce throws the jack. The club was instituted in 1859. A plaque above the pavilion door reads: 'This bowling green was the old rose garden of the ancient Manor House of Gala and was much frequented by Sir Walter Scott.'

Curling on a frozen River Tweed, 1895.

Rifle club at Mossilee, *c.* 1907. The butts show the mechanism for raising and lowering the targets.

Motor cycle race checkpoint at Albert Place, *c.* 1914.

Six Gala rugby players selected for Scotland against England on two successive Saturdays in March 1971, pictured with Provost Pate outside the Maxwell Hotel. Scotland won on both occasions. Left to right: Nairn McEwen, Duncan S. Paterson, Peter C. Brown, Provost William Pate, John Frame, Arthur Brown, Jock W.C. Turner.

PARADES & PROCESSIONS

At the Braw Lads Gathering held each summer, the elected principals, the Braw Lad and Braw Lass, and their attendants lead a cavalcade to places of interest to perform ceremonies connected with the history of the town. Here we see Braw Lad Jock Lawrie and Braw Lass May Davidson outside Wakefield Bank, Abbotsford Road, in 1939. Maypole dancing and floral parades were a prominent part of Galashiels May Queen festivities, which were held annually up to the advent of the Braw Lads Gathering in 1930.

Coronation procession, with festival queen Annie Hislop outside the Technical College, 20 June 1911.

May Queen parade in Bank Street, *c.* 1910.

An elephant draws a loaded circus wagon along the Melrose Road, *c.* 1910.

A circus parade passing the old cornmill, 1908.

King Edward VII memorial church parade, 1910. Ex-soldiers march up Galapark Road.

King Edward VII memorial church parade of Boys Brigade companies passing the Burgh School.

An entry in a cycle parade outside the Technical College, early 1900s.

Scott Street district floral fête and procession for Gala KOSB Comforts Fund, Saturday 17 July 1915. This was part of a grand children's fête and patriotic day which was held at Ladhope recreation ground. A children's choir of 400 voices was assisted by 100 ladies. The conductor was Mr J. Townley and the patriotic address was given by A.L. Brown Esq. of Galahill House.

Gala Co-op bakers in a fancy dress parade, 1924.

Gala ex-soldiers in a fancy dress parade in Galapark Road, July 1925.

Braw Lads Day celebrations in Victoria Street, 1930s.

Braw Lads Gathering with Braw Lad Jack Chapman, Braw Lass May Noble and Provost John Hayward at Abbotsford House, 1932.

The Sir Walter Scott centenary celebrations, 1932.

A crowd has gathered to cheer the Braw Lad and Lass, 1950s.

GALASHIELS AT WAR

Field-Marshal Earl Haig of Bemersyde is seen inspecting the Guard of Honour provided by the Galashiels and Selkirk Detachments of the 4th (Border) Battalion the King's Own Scottish Borderers, the KOSB, after unveiling the Galashiels War Memorial on 4 October 1925. This war memorial lists over 600 men who gave their lives for their country in the First World War. Over 3,000 men and women from the town fought or served with various branches of the armed forces during that war. Panels were added to the memorial recording those who gave their lives in the Second World War. Other photographs in this section include veterans from conflicts as far back as the Crimean War and the Indian Mutiny, to participants in both world wars, an ambulance car provided by the people of the town in 1914 and a tank which visited Galashiels in 1918.

Sergeant George Fox was a native of Galashiels and enlisted in the 42nd Regiment in 1853. He served in the Crimean War and the Indian Mutiny and later, with the 43rd Regiment, in the 1863 Maori War in New Zealand. From 1863 until he retired in 1891 he was Sergeant Instructor for the local company, the Gala Forest Rifles.

16243 Private John Richardson, 1st Battalion The Royal Scots, died of wounds on 25 June 1915, aged sixteen. Prior to enlisting he was an apprentice with M. Henry, grocer, High Street, Galashiels.

Band of the 4th KOSB outside the former Technical College in Market Street, 1910.

On 17 September 1916 a flag day was held in aid of the Scottish Veterans' Garden City Association. A stall selling flowers, vegetables, fruit and game was set up in the Corn Mill Square and proceeds went towards providing housing, training and employment for permanently disabled soldiers and sailors.

This was the first of two ambulance cars provided by the people of Galashiels for the Scottish branch of the Red Cross Society for service overseas. The 20 hp Humber (LS 413) was brought to Galashiels by Mr Adam Purves in December 1914. It was fitted with four stretchers, and could be adapted to carry eight or more patients on a folding seat on either side of the car.

Nursing Auxiliaries, 1940s.

In November 1915 the Galashiels
Branch of the Vegetable Products
Committee was formed and opened a
depot in the Station Yard. It despatched
fresh fruit and vegetables to the Fleet,
and was open on Tuesdays from 11 a.m.
until 2 p.m. The goods were despatched
the same afternoon by train. The porter
in the photograph is Dave Henderson.

Children of the Burgh School collect pots and pans for the war effort.

The Tank 'bank' Julian arrived by train on Sunday night, 6 October 1918, and was opened for business the following day at the Corn Mill Square. Investments were made at the Burgh Buildings. Investors then had their war bonds and war saving certificates impressed with the tank bank's stamp. At the close of business £57,300 worth of War Bonds and War Saving Certificates had been purchased. During the week the tank visited other Border towns.

On 24 October 1918 a plane crash-landed at Kilnknowe, Galashiels.

During the First World War the YMCA rooms in the High Street, with facilities for reading, writing and games, were well patronised by the large number of soldiers billeted in the town. Evening services were held on Sundays.

Tommy Waddell and RAF comrades in Belfast, during the Second World War.

Ex-Servicemen in the wool trade in New South Wales collected £1,100 for the purchase of 2,200 parcels which they requested should be distributed to needy people linked with the wool trade in Scotland, Yorkshire and the west of England. On 1 September 1949 the local distribution of the food gifts took place at the Lucy Sanderson Homes where Mrs R.S. Hayward, one of the governors of the homes, handed out parcels.

Fifth Ward entertaining the war wounded, outside the Technical College.

Observer Corps, No. 6 crew.

Home Guard A Co. No. 2, pictured in front of the Town Hall.

On 26 February 1908 a presentation was made in the Drill Hall in recognition of service by the Galashiels Crimean and Indian Mutiny Veterans. This photograph was taken a few weeks before the presentation, which only four of the original seven veterans attended. John Morrison died on 30 January and Messrs Nichol and Brownlee could not attend owing to illness. Standing, left to right: Sgt.-Maj. Rodgers, Pte. Hobson. Seated: Sgt. Nichol, Pte. Morrison, Pte. Brownlee, Cpl. Inglis, Pte. Foley.

Gavin Richardson gave a talk in 1985 at Old Gala House on the KOSB in Gallipoli in 1915. He is seen here with three veterans, left to right: George Waugh 1/4th KOSB, Jimmy Heron MM, 1/4th KOSB and Jock McKerlie 1/5th KOSB.

MANSION HOUSES

Galashiels had its own manor house, Old Gala House, which in its present form dates from the late sixteenth century. Many of the largest mansion houses in the area date from the nineteenth century, however. Hugh Scott, Laird of Gala, built New Gala House, shown here, in 1876 at a cost of £25,000. This magnificent building was demolished in 1987. Families who had made their fortunes in India found the area attractive and quite convenient for Edinburgh. They built houses such as Bowland House and Langlee House. Other substantial houses were erected by local industrialists, Glenmayne House and Fairnilee House being good examples, while Peel House was the home of an Edinburgh merchant.

Old Gala House, the oldest building in Galashiels. There has been a manor house on this site since 1457, although the present house dates from 1583, with additions made in 1611, 1700, 1760 and 1830. Old Gala House was the home of the Lairds of Gala – the Pringle family – until 1632, then the Scotts of Gala until the family moved to New Gala House. In 1948 the house was purchased by Gala Arts Association who in turn passed it on to Galashiels Town Council in 1974.

The drawing room in Old Gala House, c. 1890.

Torwoodlee, *c.* 1878. The house was built in 1783 as the home of the Pringle family. The main entrance was moved to the other side of the house in 1864, to maintain privacy following the construction of The Birks on the opposite side of the valley.

Bowland House was built on the site of a medieval manor house of the Archbishop of St Andrews. The present house dates largely from 1811 when additions were made to the seventeenth-century mansion for the Walker family. Further additions were made to the rear of the building in 1890.

Galashiels Ex-Service Pipe Band playing at Gala House. Drum Major, Jock Lyall and Pipe Major Marshall.

Langlee House was for many years the seat of the Dalrymple family, who had trading interests in India and Fife. The house was demolished in the 1960s.

Peel House, *c.* 1920. The house was built in 1908 by Mr Ovens, bought by Lord Craigmyle and given to the nation as a military hospital in 1939. As well as servicemen, children from London suffering from tuberculosis were sent to Peel Hospital. After the war the hospital developed into a general hospital with 220 beds until replaced by Borders District General Hospital, near Melrose, in 1988; although unused at present, the house is still standing.

Fairnilee House gardens, *c.* 1968. The house was built in 1904–6 for D.F. Roberts, a Selkirk textile manufacturer. Nearby are the ruins of Old Fairnilee, a sixteenth-century mansion.

Glenmayne House, designed by Edinburgh architect David Bryce, was built in 1866 at a cost of £20,000 for John Murray of Sanderson and Murray, Buckholmside, pelt mongers.

Threepwood Mansion, early 1900s. The old spelling 'Thriepwood' means 'disputed land'. As a few different parish boundaries meet here, it is possible there were disputed borders.

RURAL

Galashiels, with its weekly market, was the centre of a prosperous agricultural area. The town held an agricultural show in the Gala Policies, now the Scott Park, until the late 1930s. This was a big event during the summer and the townsfolk would line St John Street to watch the livestock arriving. Entries for the event included horses, especially Clydesdales and hunters, sheep, dairy cows, pigeons and rabbits. A display of horse jumping was held in the afternoon with musical interludes from Gala Town Band. This section depicts some aspects of the countryside and country life in the vicinity. Shown here is Ellwyn Glen, which in times past was a popular place for picnics especially the Fairy Dean, where 'fairy stones' from the burn were supposed to bring good luck. At one time seven bridges crossed the stream in the glen.

Cauldshiels Loch, 'The Bleak Lake'. Until Sir Walter Scott planted trees on the Abbotsford side of the loch it was entirely without shelter. In the extremely cold winter of 1895 the loch was reputed to be frozen over and traversed by a gentleman in his horse and carriage.

The Eildons from Melrose Road. Close to this spot now is a plaque bearing the inscription: 'At this spot on his pathetic journey from Italy home to Abbotsford and his beloved Border Land, Sir Walter Scott gazing on this scene for the last time "sprang up with a cry of delight" – 11 July 1832.'

Bringing in the hay, late 1950s.

Harvesting at Caddonlee, 1913. The photograph was taken from 'Luggie Field' with Caddonlee Hill in the background. On the extreme left is Robert Logan, the farmer. The farm is now run by the Pate family.

Clovenfords, *c.* 1860. The Hearse Society shed and old police station are on the left. The road is the old highway between Selkirk and Edinburgh.

Clovenfords Hotel, with Sir Walter Scott's statue in the forecourt. The original inn dates back to about 1750, and was an important stop for stage coaches en route from Edinburgh to Carlisle. Sir Walter Scott stayed here in 1799 prior to taking a lease on Ashiestiel House nearby. When stagecoach travel ceased in about 1833 the inn became two cottages, Whytbanklee Cottages, until 1901, when the building reverted to a hotel. The inn was also visited by William and Dorothy Wordsworth, and John Ruskin.

Traffic hold-up on a country road.

Penning the sheep at Lindean Moor.

Thrashing on a Borders farm, *c.* 1936. Note the number of workers needed to carry out this seasonal task.

Colin Wood driving a McCormack binder and Peter Wood on a Field Marshal Crawler tractor at work in the field next to Ladhope Golf Course, early 1950s.

The Lauderdale Foxhounds on Langshaw Road with Huntsman Will White, 1958.

Langshaw Folk Group at the Palais de Dance, Fountainbridge, Edinburgh, *c.* 1935.

A shepherd carrying a lamb in his traditional plaid.

Rounding up the stragglers at tea time.

George Hardie sharpening his scythe ready for a
day's work.

A helicopter at Lodge Field, Bowland, assisting with the supply of feed to livestock during the severe
winter of 1963.

ACKNOWLEDGEMENTS

We would like to thank the many people who have kindly contributed to the Old Gala Club photographic collection over the years.

This publication represents only a small part of our collection of approximately 4,000 photographs which is housed in Galashiels Public Library and catalogued by the club's photographic group.

We are indebted to the following for allowing us to use copyright material:

Border Telegraph, Galashiels
Southern Reporter, Selkirk
Waverley Studios, Galashiels
Ian Mitchell, for R. Clapperton, Photographers, Selkirk
Mrs Chick & Miss M. Edwards, for Edwards, Photographers, Selkirk

Final thanks go to Helen Elliott, Gavin Richardson and Ian Miller for enabling this book to come to fruition.

BRITAIN IN OLD PHOTOGRAPHS

To order any of these titles please telephone our distributor, Littlehampton Book Services on 01903 721596
For a catalogue of these and our other titles please ring Regina Schinner on 01453 731114